IMAGES OF ENGLAND

BIGGLESWADE

T0347021

IMAGES OF ENGLAND

BIGGLESWADE

KEN PAGE

The
History
Press

Frontispiece: Biggleswade windmill, *c.* 1930.

First published 2006

Reprinted in 2014 by
The History Press
The Mill, Brimscombe Port,
Stroud, Gloucestershire, GL5 2QG
www.thehistorypress.co.uk

British Library Cataloguing in Publication Data.
A catalogue record for this book is available from the British Library.

ISBN 978 0 7524 3766 8

Printed in Great Britain.

Contents

Descriptions of Biggleswade

Thy road, my Biggleswade, deserving draws
From the pleas'd traveller his just applause;
Nor less the lucid stream that laves thy side,
Deck'd in the flowing pomp of ready pride;
Whether for gain, or in the finny line,
For on thy eels, good gods, how we did dine!
Thomas Maude, eighteenth century

Pleasantly situated on the Ivel and furnished with commodious Inns.
Revd Thomas Cox, Magna Britannia, 1715

One of the greatest markets in England for barley.
Daniel Defoe, 1724

Biggleswade, the next market town we visited, is situated in a most pleasant manner, on the banks of the river Ivel, over which there is a good stone bridge and lighters come up with coal to the town.
N. Spencer, Complete English Traveller, 1772

Biggleswade after all for my money, with its young
Rabbits, and silver eels; and a sandy flat soil to ride upon.
Hon. John Byng, June 1792

The Church was built in 1230. The parishioners are free tenants and all have equal rights to any of the seats. Thus should it ever be. In the sight of god all distinctions are levelled. For this privilege however the inhabitants are constrained to repair and rebuild the church where necessary.
F.W. Brayley and J. Britton, Beauties of England and Wales, 1801

The neat and respectable appearance of this town may in a great measure be ascribed to a terrible fire that happened upon the 16th June 1785.
Edward Mogg, Patersons Roads, 1829

With the revival of the popularity of the road in the pursuit of that healthful and enjoyable exercise, cycling, a new era of prosperity has set in for the old town … now the favourite rendezvous of wheelmen from all parts on tour through the district.
Illustrated Bedfordshire, 1895

The town can boast its fair share of the eighteenth century red-brick fronts and doorways which form the chief attraction of so many country places.
Victoria County History, 1908

A thriving market town, centre for much market gardening, especially in cucumbers and pickling onions.
H.W. Macklin, Bedfordshire & Huntingdonshire, 1917

Every motorist knows its wide street and splendid market place on the Great North Road.
Arthur Mee, The King's England, 1939

Acknowledgements

The text and captions were written by Ken Page and checked by Eric Lund and Mike Strange, with other team members David and Peter Parker. The photographs are taken from collections held by Biggleswade History Society, who may be contacted through their website: www. biggleswadehistory.org.uk.

Introduction

Situated in the Ivel Valley, Biggleswade is an ancient market town. By 1066 there were three manors, Biggleswade, Stratton and Holme. The town was Pichelsuuade, (Bichels Ford) in the Domesday Book of 1086. There was a bridge over the river Ivel by the fourteenth century and the present Ivel Bridge was rebuilt in 2000. Recent excavations at Stratton Park revealed an Anglo-Saxon and medieval settlement. Holme, from the Old Norse *holm* (island), was absorbed into Biggleswade by 1660. The manor of Stratton came into the Cotton family by marriage early in the seventeenth century. The Barnett family was the last to hold the manor and the estate was sold in 1910. The Manor House was demolished in 1960.

King Henry I granted the manor of Biggleswade and Holme in 1132 to Bishop Hugh of Lincoln. In 1227 King Henry III confirmed the market originally granted by King John. By 1631 there were five annual fairs. The ancient Horse Fair on 14 February lasted until 1958. There were corn, straw plait and livestock markets until the twentieth century. The Market Square contained a shambles burned down in 1896 when the square was opened up; there was redevelopment in 1937 when the ancient Market House was reconstructed using original timber framing. A new enhancement scheme was completed in 2003 with the restoration of a granite drinking fountain originally installed in 1908 as a memorial to Queen Victoria.

The present parish church of St Andrew dates back to the thirteenth century, but there is evidence of a previous Saxon church on the site. Mary Tealby, the founder of Battersea Dogs' Home, is buried in the churchyard. A variety of religious buildings have existed, including a Quaker Meeting House burned down during a large fire in 1783. The Old Meeting Baptist chapel was destroyed in the Great Fire of 1785 but soon rebuilt and replaced with a modern church in 1968. The first Methodist chapel came in 1795 and the present chapel opened in 1834. A Catholic chapel opened in 1905, moving to a church in 1936 and again to a modern church in 1973.

The early Great North Road from London to Edinburgh came through the town and it was in a bad state before being turnpiked from Stevenage in 1720 and to Alconbury in 1725. A third turnpike road from Stratton to Ramsey started at the Spread Eagle Inn (now Eagle Farm Road) in 1754 and is now the B1040 to Crowland in Lincolnshire. Many inns and taverns were developed in the early part of the seventeenth century to cope with the expanding coaching trade along the road. The A1 passed right through the town until a bypass was constructed in 1961.

In 1758 the river Ivel was made navigable from Biggleswade to Kings Lynn. Three wharfs were built to unload and distribute goods such as coal and timber to the surrounding district.

There were twenty-six maltings in the town converting local barley to malt supplied to London via Kings Lynn and the North Sea. In 1823 the navigation extended to Shefford. There were two watermills; Ivel Mill suffered a serious fire in 1945 and was converted into flats in 1982. Holme Mills, the only remaining working mill in Bedfordshire, is now producing Jordan's breakfast cereals. The largest and finest windmill in Bedfordshire, built in 1860, was 70ft high but was demolished in 1967. There was also a steam mill on the same site until 1977.

Samuel Wells established Biggleswade Brewery in 1764; this became the Greene King brewery in 1961 and closed down in 1997. The town suffered a setback with the Great Fire of 1785 when part of the town was destroyed, including 9 maltings and 103 houses, making 332 people homeless. Thankfully, no lives were lost. The town soon recovered but it was not until 1874 that a volunteer fire service was formed, changing from a horse-drawn steamer to a motor fire engine in 1928. It was nationalised in 1941 but in 1948 became part of the Bedfordshire Fire Service.

The Great Northern Railway from London to Peterborough arrived in 1850. By then the population had risen from less than 800 in 1671 to nearly 5,000. The railway gave market gardeners access to London markets for their fresh vegetables. Trainloads of horse manure were carried back from London to enrich the soil. Unsanitary conditions existed in many of the overcrowded areas and yards in the town. Biggleswade Water Board started pumping water to the town in 1907 from the well at New Spring, but sewage systems were not fully developed until 1912. Slum clearance schemes made way for new building from the 1930s. A large number of council houses were built from 1914 right up to the 1970s.

Dan Albone (1860-1906) was a local inventor and champion cyclist, renowned for early cycles and cars and internationally credited with manufacturing the first practical lightweight tractor – the Ivel Agricultural Motor – in 1902. Maythorn & Co., which was established in 1842 and built horse carriages, expanded into making bodies for luxury motor cars in their Market Square plant. The factory was rebuilt after a spectacular fire in 1923, but closed down in 1931. Kayser Bondor manufactured ladies' stockings and lingerie for many years. Many other large engineering works came to Biggleswade from 1939 to 1945, such as Weatherley Oilgear Ltd (later Cincinnati Milacron), Pobjoy Airmotors & Aircraft, and Smart & Brown Machine Tools Ltd. Berkeley Caravans and Cars were nationally known in the 1960s; the three-wheeled version is much sought after by collectors. The main industrial site today attracting more factories and warehousing is at Stratton Business Park.

Edward Peake set up a school in 1557 but modern education began in 1874 with the British School in Rose Lane, followed by two church schools. Now there are numerous schools controlled by the county council.

Charles Penrose (1874-1952), was born in the High Street and had a long career in film, theatre and radio. He released his first gramophone record in 1911, and his most famous, *The Laughing Policeman*, was recorded in 1936. The Pre-Raphaelite painter Henry Ryland (1856-1924), was born in Hitchin Street.

Many new houses were constructed after 1945 and there has been a steady growth in population, accelerated in the 1990s with the start of large developments to the east of the town. With the population now well over 15,000, many more houses are planned in the Kings Reach development. Many residents commute to work and have ready access to the A1 plus half-hourly trains to London and Peterborough and a regular bus service to nearby towns and villages.

Ken Page
October 2005

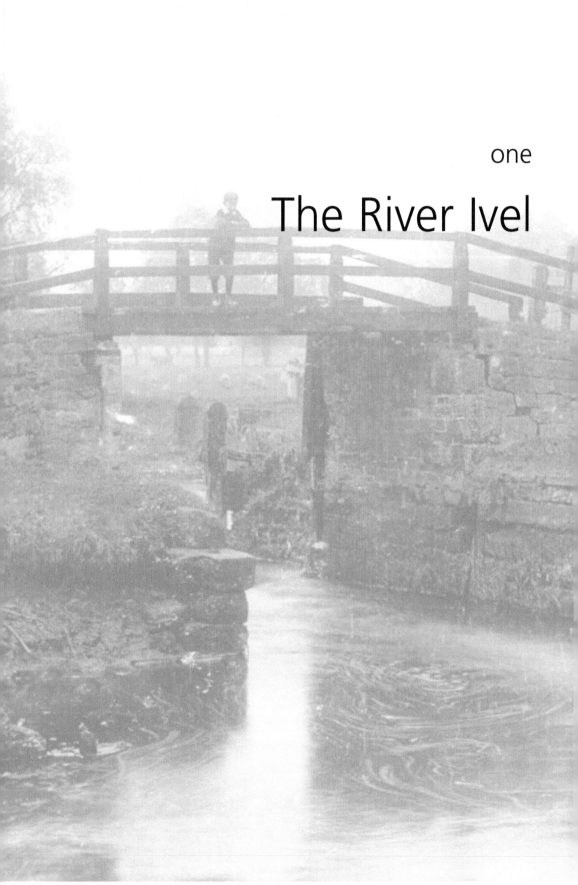

one

The River Ivel

Holme Mills in 1896 after being converted into a roller mill. The Ivel Navigation opened in 1759 from Biggleswade through to Kings Lynn and extended to Shefford in 1823, closing in 1876.

Holme Mills was rebuilt after a fire in 1899 and is seen here, together with the miller's house, in 1905. It is now the only working mill in Bedfordshire.

Above and below: A 10-ton steam ploughing engine fell into the lock at Holme Mills on 11 February 1873, dropping 18ft into the river. Two enginemen were fatally injured.

Above and below: Biggleswade Windmill around 1900 (*above*) and around 1930 (*below*). Built in 1858, it was the tallest (70ft) and finest in Bedfordshire and, although it was a listed building, it was demolished in 1967.

By 1913 boys were able to bathe in the river, where a basic corrugated iron bathing shed was available for changing.

Boating was an enjoyable summer pastime during the First World War. Ivel Meadow, later the Franklin Recreation Ground, is on the left.

The riverside was further developed into a popular lido from 1929 to 1939, when it closed due to the Second World War, never to reopen.

The riverside walk and Franklin Recreation Ground soon after it opened in 1924. Henry Franklin, the miller, gave the meadow to the town.

The riverside footpath and Mill Lock from the mill bridge, *c.* 1900. This was then, as now, a popular walk for townsfolk.

Franklin's Mill, seen here around 1910, was mentioned in the Domesday Book of 1086. Ivel House was built in 1898 for the miller. After a disastrous fire at the mill in 1945, it was only used for storage. The mill was converted into flats in 1982.

Before the Ivel Navigation was extended to Shefford, lighters were turned at the mill pit. It was filled in and grassed over in the early 1970s.

There has been a riverside walk using the former hauling way ever since the Ivel Navigation closed in 1876. From Franklin's Mill, the Back Meadows lead to the Ivel Bridge.

The attractive sandstone Ivel Bridge replaced an earlier wooden structure in 1796.

The bridge was replaced by twin 'Meccano' bridges between 1940 and 1948. A new concrete bridge was completed in 2001.

The Black Locks beside Biggleswade Common (the largest area of open grassland in Bedfordshire) were blown up during the First World War to provide more arable land for the war effort.

The Northern Signal Companies of the Royal Engineers were stationed at nearby Fairfield during 1914-15 and often watered their horses at the river.

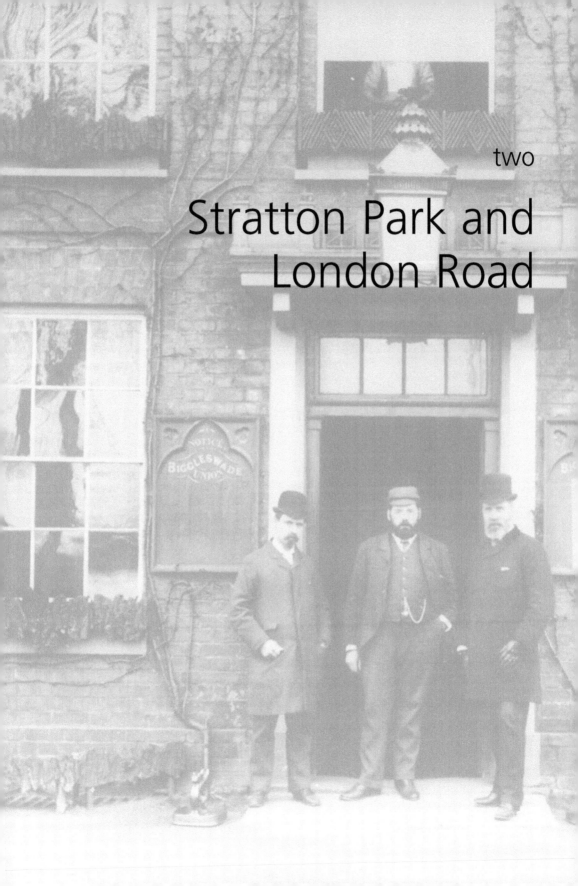

two

Stratton Park and London Road

The Great North Road (A1) was originally a Roman road running through Biggleswade until the bypass opened in 1961. The water tower on Topler's Hill opened in 1934.

Opposite below: The only bomb damage inflicted at Biggleswade was in 1940 at New Spring Cottages next to the pumping station. There were no fatalities and Civil Defence Workers are seen here clearing up the mess. Other bombs were dropped in open ground at Stratton Park and on the Common.

Above: At the bottom of Topler's Hill is the original pumping station built of local sandstone, which was opened in 1906 to draw water from an artesian well dug at New Spring in 1902. It is 176ft deep and 10ft in diameter. Capable of pumping 1 million gallons of water a day, the well is still in operation.

The Manor House of Stratton dates back to Saxon times. Captain Charles Fitz Roy Barnett (*left*), the last of his line, died in 1897 and Lucy Jane (*right*) his wife, in 1908. W.B. Micklethwaite photographed them around 1870.

The Elizabethan Manor House was refaced in the nineteenth century using local bricks carted by farmers and market gardeners on the estate.

There were extensive gardens at the Manor House. When the Stratton estate was sold in 1910, it comprised 1,070 acres, including several farms and smallholdings. Bedfordshire County Council purchased most of the land.

A short distance from the Manor House, Stratton Lodge was the dower house originally used by members of the Barnett family.

Above and below: The mansion became Parkfield School; pupils and teachers are seen here in 1930. The mansion was used by the Army from 1939–45 and lastly as a battery chicken factory before being demolished in 1960.

The delightful Dunton Lane, running through the manor of Stratton, is much changed since this photograph was taken around 1900.

Charlie Ferguson (*left*), seen here in 1910, ran a riding school and taxi service. He is pictured at the bottom of Topler's Hill with his new motor taxi, talking to one of his riding staff.

Biggleswade Union Workhouse was completed in 1836 to accommodate 280 inmates from twenty-two parishes. This photograph shows the workhouse after a new wing was added in 1893.

Workhouse Master Charles Guy (centre) with Mr French and Mr Ellwood, two members of the board of guardians, outside the entrance to Biggleswade Union Workhouse in 1893.

An aerial view of London Road in the 1960s, with the workhouse site outlined.

Mantle's Garage in London Road started with the wooden building in 1920 and is still expanding. This 1928 photograph shows a telegraph pole and sewage breather pipe being moved to a more convenient site.

The turnpike road from Biggleswade to St Ives and Ramsey opened in 1754, starting from the Spread Eagle on the Great North Road. The inn later became Eagle Farm (pictured above) and was demolished in 1960. The present B1040 road starts at Drove Road and continues to Crowland in Lincolnshire.

Eagle Farm Road leads to Stratton Grammar School, shown here soon after opening in 1950. It is now Biggleswade Upper School.

three

Stratton Street, High Street and Market Square

The Red Lion, seen here in 1961, is an ancient public house still operating on the southern end of the original manor of Biggleswade. The external studding was added after 1905.

Looking back from Stratton Street to the Red Lion, c. 1905. At this time, it was not fashionable to expose timber framing. Leading up to the railway bridge are Victorian houses, the Bay Horse beerhouse and thatched cottages.

Above and below: Looking up to (*above*) and down from (*below*) the railway bridge around 1900. In this area there was a collection of public houses, business premises and shops leading down to the Market Square.

A funeral procession headed by the Royal Engineers band, *c.* 1915. It is passing Goldthorpe's ironmongers, which is still trading and is almost unchanged in character.

Postal and telegraph staff in front of the High Street post office in 1896. The post office moved to Station Road in 1900.

Above and below: Two views of the Market Shambles after they burned down in 1896. They were demolished and not replaced.

The spacious Market Square was developed between 1190 and 1200. This engraving of 1855 shows the town pump and lantern with the ancient sixteenth-century Market House behind. The Swan Hotel bus conveys guests from the railway station.

The Market Square had been opened out by 1897. Here, walkers perambulate around the new drinking fountain in front of the Market House.

The High Street and Market Square, showing the drum clock on the post office. Following complaints from the postmaster that the clock winder had to pass through his bedroom to wind the clock, it was removed to the Town Hall in 1898.

The Town Hall and drum clock in 1910. A thirsty market gardeners' horse is drinking at the trough provided for this purpose.

The drinking fountain in Market Square was built to commemorate the reign of Queen Victoria and the Coronation of King Edward VII. It was opened on 14 October 1908. The monument was removed during improvements in 1937 and restored in various locations. Much was missing when it was restored in 2003.

Joseph Wren and son, fishmongers and poulterers, stand in the doorway of their Market Square shop on 4 June 1892. On the right is the entrance to the New Inn Yard, where the pig market was held.

Shop assistants pose outside Soundy's millinery, drapery and shoe shop on the Square in the 1930s.

Larkinson's Fancy Goods store in High Street was a 200-year-old building adapted for the 1930s with an art deco front. The front is decked out for the Coronation of King George VI in 1937.

The Market Square in 1930. Herbert Church had opened his furniture emporium with a canopy over the pavement. The urban district council purchased the canopy area (originally a garden) in 1935 after the shop closed.

E.D. Fisher & Sons ironmongery took over the old established business, which included an iron foundry, in 1904 and continued until 1978.

A typical busy Saturday market, *c.* 1960. A similar scene can still be seen on the Square today. The Market House (*right*) was completely reconstructed in 1937 using the original wooden framing.

Ox-roasting outside the Town Hall to celebrate the Coronation of King Edward VII in 1902.

When the Boer War ended in 1902 there were joyful celebrations, with vast crowds assembling on the Market Square.

Dense crowds attend the proclamation of King George V outside the Town Hall in 1910.

People gather in the Market Square for George V's Silver Jubilee celebrations in 1935.

Above: As part of the 1935 Silver Jubilee celebrations, afternoon tea was provided for children at numerous venues; these children are proceeding past the war memorial to the Conservative Hall.

A line-up of local dignitaries, with the Sea Cadet buglers, at the proclamation of Queen Elizabeth II in 1952.

The war memorial was consecrated in 1921 at the junction of High Street, Shortmead Street and St Andrews Street. It remained here until 1977, when it was moved to the Market Square to ease traffic congestion.

Opposite below: Dancing in the Market Square as part of the joyous celebrations on VE (Victory in Europe) Day in 1945.

The war memorial in 1925. Humphries & Edwards jewellers premises, on the right, is where Charles Penrose (1874-1952), made famous by his 1926 record *The Laughing Policeman*, was born; the shop was owned by his father.

St Andrew's Place, an ancient building leading into Shortmead Street, probably started as two tithe barns in the churchyard. Whiteman & Sons cycle dealers and repairers traded here for many years.

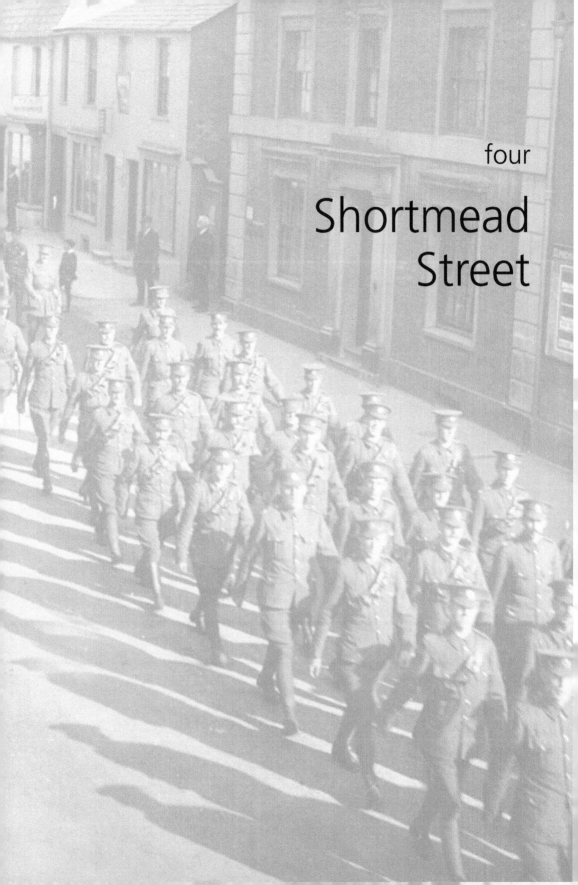

four

Shortmead
Street

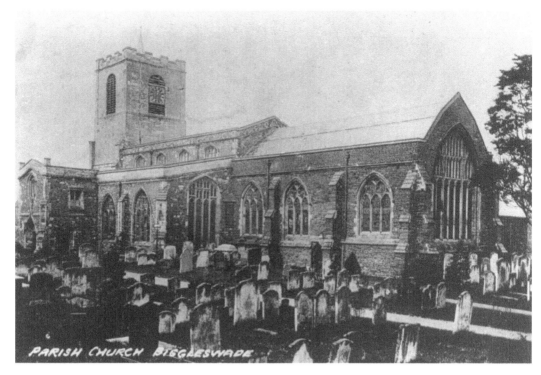

St Andrew's parish church, viewed from Shortmead Street, 1910. The church dates back to at least 1276 and most likely replaced a Saxon building.

Looking east from the Back Meadows, where sheep grazed, and across the river to St Andrew's church and Shortmead Street.

Above and below: The parish church before and after 1920, when miller Henry Franklin presented the rood screen to the church in memory of his son who perished in the First World War.

The Victorian vicarage next to St Andrew's church was built around 1850, but by 1969 it was considered uneconomic to retain and replaced with a new building.

This everyday scene in Shortmead Street around 1910 shows a typical market town on the Great North Road.

Flooding in Shortmead Street, *c.* 1905. As the street was close to the river, floods were commonplace.

The Royal Engineers march along Shortmead Street from their base at Fairfield for Church Parade in 1915.

Above: Shop assistants pose outside the *Biggleswade Chronicle* offices in 1925. The *Biggleswade Chronicle* was established in 1890 and shortly afterwards they moved to premises in Shortmead Street. The proprietor, Charles Elphick, also sold stationery, toys and fancy goods. The central passage leads to the printing works. The newspaper continues today after several changes of ownership. The building has now been converted into flats.

The Wesleyan chapel, 1920. It was built in 1834 and is now the Trinity Methodist church.

Above: Ebenezer Dew's horse bus, built by John Maythorn, outside the Coach and Horses in 1878. Ebenezer Dew was licensee of the Coach and Horses and also a local carrier. Thomas Dew, Ebenezer's father, started the business and it was carried on by Ebenezer's son William until 1948. The cottage on the right has recently been restored.

Opposite below: Beaumont Close was built in 1840 for merchant John Foster. It was adapted as a nursing home in 1987.

A line of shops opposite the Coach and Horses in 1937, comprising a stationer's, a pawnbroker's, a hardware store, a basket-maker and a butcher's.

Above: An interesting scene at the north end of Shortmead Street, *c.* 1920. A chimney sweep's house, a family doctor's surgery and the Drill Hall can be seen on the left. On the right is a baker's shop, a passageway leading to one of numerous yards, and the Peacock beerhouse. Territorial soldiers, a motor car, a market gardener's cart and the Royal Oak Hotel are visible in the background.

Opposite: Digging the main sewer in Shortmead Street, reputed to be the oldest road in Biggleswade, in 1908. The busy junction is closed and sightseers, mainly children, are watching in fascination.

Sheldon & Blake motor engineers opened one of the first garages in 1920, later becoming the North Road Auto Co. The building is still in use today selling used cars.

A market gardener with his cart at the northern boundary of Biggleswade, at Bells Brook. The Lion beerhouse, in the background, is actually in Northill parish.

Residents flock to watch the Royal Engineers entering Biggleswade on 21 August 1914.

A short distance from Shortmead Street, St John's church was built in 1833, designed by
Sir A.W. Bloomfield with 420 seats and three bells. Pictured in 1920, it was demolished in
1975. The site is now a block of maisonettes.

At the end of Fairfield Road are two mansions with different histories. Shortmead House (*above*) was Shortmead Farm in 1765 and was considerably altered in Victorian times. Fairfield House (*below*) was built around 1833 for Robert Lindsell. Henry Lindsell owned both estates when he died in 1925. They were sold separately but Fairfield Meadow was bequeathed conditionally to the town of Biggleswade.

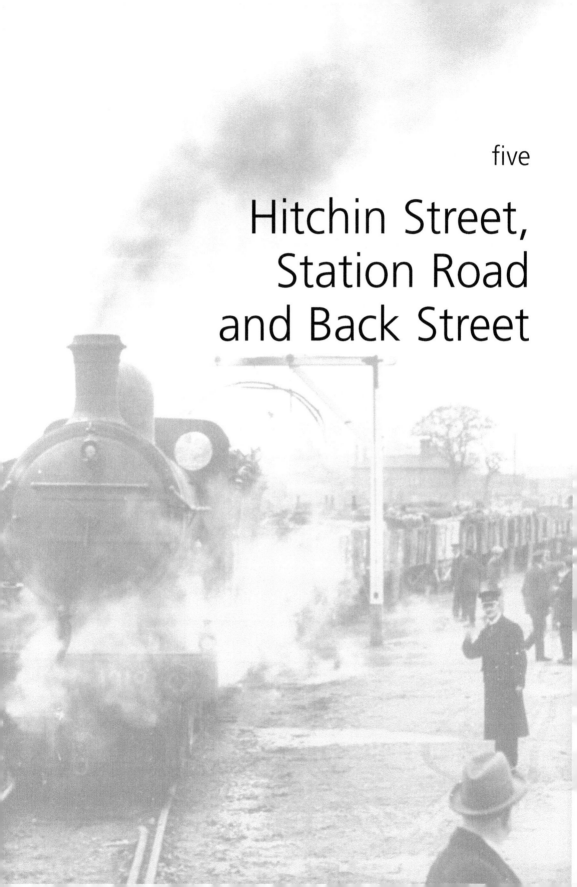

five

Hitchin Street,
Station Road
and Back Street

This butcher's shop was built on the site of the George Inn, which burned down in the Great Fire of 1785. George Bygraves, the butcher, is in the centre with his son beside him. Displaying meat outside was not considered unhygienic in 1892. Household deliveries were made daily on horseback. Next door is Richard Swift's Market Square grocer's shop and a group of small boys are watching the photographer.

Looking along Hitchin Street, 1906. The butcher's shop is now a household store and opposite is the barber's shop of 'Professor' Page.

International Stores advertised themselves as 'The Greatest Grocers in the World' and by 1894 traded at No. 7 Hitchin Street. The employees are pictured in 1907.

Next door to the International Stores was the draper's shop owned by Mrs Saunderson, seen here with her daughter Matilda outside the shop around 1907.

Hitchin Street is thronged with thankful people during peace celebrations in 1919.

The friendly wartime Ministry of Labour and National Service office staff pose outside a converted Hitchin Street shop in the 1940s. The Ministry of Labour was the forerunner of today's Job Centre.

John Bond was a baker at The Granary on the corner of Bonds Lane, which was named after him. The premises, seen here in 1970, are now a café and the surrounding shops are continually changing.

Alfred Wakes' bakers shop was on the corner of Hitchin Street and Mill Lane. Alfred's son, Douglas, is on his way to deliver fresh bread to local customers around 1925.

Joe Wren, the fishmonger, walked the town with his fresh fish daily and Hitchin Street was part of his weekly route in 1928.

Maurice Smith, a local dairyman, was a familiar sight with his ice cream tricycle in 1928. He later expanded his business.

The Empire cinema, built for travelling showman Charles Thurston, is seen here soon after it opened in 1913. It closed in 1958, being converted into an electronics factory, and is now Empire Close, a residential development.

James Harris, the local showman, with his funfair in the Dolphin Meadow next to the Empire cinema, c. 1914. The meadow later became the cattle market and is now part of Empire Close.

Left: Thomas Course, a local millwright, opened his works in 1846. By 1970 the building was used for metal hardening and brazing. It was recently demolished to make way for five new maisonettes.

Below: Factory units appeared at the end of Hitchin Street with Eldon Way and Albone Way being constructed by 1970. The former Nags Head pub is now residential.

Opposite above: Brittain's Furnishers traded at the old Drill Hall in Palace Street in the 1930s. The first Baptist church on this site was burned down in 1785. It is now derelict and awaiting redevelopment.

Opposite below: The general post office moved from High Street to Station Road in 1900. It was rebuilt in 1982.

Above: Police Constable Tom Paxton stands at the door of the police station in Station Road, just after it was built in 1938. It is still operational.

Opposite: The Providence Strict Baptist chapel stood in Back Street for 150 years, until it was demolished in 1987 to make way for retirement flats.

The Great Northern Railway came to Biggleswade in 1850 and this is the original railway station in 1892.

Above: A new railway station, still in daily use, opened in 1900 when the line was increased to four tracks.

Opposite above: A familiar scene in the 1920s. Market gardeners' carts are lined up along Station Road; the first one is on the weighbridge. A sign of impending change is the motor lorry.

Opposite below: The special London & North Eastern Railway goods train leaves for Covent Garden market in London; fresh vegetables will be on sale there early the next morning. Another train is also being loaded, possibly for Sheffield market.

A4 locomotive *Empire of India* travelling north at speed in 1938. From 1935 streamline trains passed through Biggleswade daily on the LNER East Coast main line.

The 9.1 (09.01) morning train to Kings Cross was the first non-stop local train from Biggleswade to London. in 1946 the modernised A3 Pacific *St Simon* gets a clear signal.

six

Brewing, Malting and Pubs

Left and below: Two views of the Wells & Co. brewery in 1873. The front of the brewery (*above*) was in Brewery Lane, now Church Street, and the rear (*left*) was in Hicks Pits. Samuel Wells established the Biggleswade Brewery in 1764.

Opposite below: Wells & Winch Ltd was registered in 1899, and the brewery was rebuilt by 1901 with a view to expand. They amalgamated with Greene King & Sons Ltd in 1961. The brewery closed in 1997.

Above: The Kings Arms Inn in High Street and brewery behind in Church Street were purchased by Samuel Wells in 1764 and soon converted into offices. It was here that Samuel Wells opened the Biggleswade Bank in 1830. Wells & Co. sold it in 1893 to Capital & Counties Bank. This 1892 photograph shows the Georgian bank on the left, with the adjoining manager's house. The premises are now Lloyds TSB bank.

The Coronation of King George V in 1911 was celebrated with a parade through the town. One of several Wells & Winch horse drays is in the brewery yard waiting to move off.

A group of contented brewery workers in the yard in 1914, with a dray in the background. The brewery cat was very important to control rats and mice.

The first Commer lorry in the 1920s, with solid tyres, in front of a new block of garages.

The brewery expanded over the years. The fleet of lorries, seen here in 1934, includes some from several other breweries which had been taken over.

Harold Darnell and Walter Day take a breather after unloading casks from their big Commer lorry in 1938.

This 12-ton Foden lorry with a very obvious theme entered in the 1949 Biggleswade Carnival.

The brewery football team had a very successful 1949/50 season. The team represented most of the departments.

A happy group of wartime bottling ladies in 1940, when women made up a large proportion of the brewery workforce. With restrictions on raw materials, beer was in short supply and in the summer pubs rapidly sold out of their weekly allocation.

There were twenty-six maltings in Biggleswade during the eighteenth century. Malt was carried along the Ivel and Ouse Navigations to Kings Lynn and by sea to London. Ebenezer Chew took this photograph of Franklin's Malting in St Andrew's Street on 2 February 1895.

Downs Maltings (now the Old Maltings) in Church Street. John Larkinson, the maltster, is seen here with his family outside the maltster's cottage in the 1890s.

The Royal Oak" in the 19th Century

Your host   GEORGE PILBOROUGH will welcome you at

"The Royal Oak" Hotel   SUN STREET
BIGGLESWADE, Beds.

Telephone: Biggleswade 2264

Above and below: Biggleswade was prominent on the Great North Road and was a recognised coaching stop with numerous inns, taverns and public houses opening over the years. Fifty-two public houses were recorded in 1876. Two ancient coaching inns, the Royal Oak and the Sun, stood side by side in Sun Street.

Above and below: The Swan and the Crown were coaching inns standing opposite each other in High Street. They were destroyed in 1785 during the Great Fire of Biggleswade. They were rebuilt by 1800 and are shown here in the early twentieth century.

Horses and drivers enjoy a lunch break at the Yorkshire Grey in London Road, which was purpose-built next to the workhouse on a field called Gallows Piece in 1836.

Members of the darts club enjoy a yard of ale contest at the Yorkshire Grey in 1957.

Above: The Gardeners Arms, Potton Road in 1920 with the licensee's family. This was originally an unnamed beerhouse in an adapted private house.

The timber-framed White Hart, built around 1639, is the oldest building in Biggleswade after the parish church. This 1915 scene shows the Royal Naval Air Service motorised artillery formed to shoot down German Zeppelins. Looking into the White Hart yard are mansard-roofed cottages, a steam-engine works and wooden outbuildings, all long gone.

The Old Spread Eagle in Potton Road, near a new council housing estate, was rebuilt in 1938.

Opposite below: The George Hotel was built in 1856 to serve railway passengers. Landlord William Parker was also a coal merchant. This photograph was taken in 1956; the hotel closed in 1965.

Above and below: The Old Spread Eagle dressed up for the Coronation of Queen Elizabeth in 1953. After 1961 it became a Greene King pub, closing in 1997. There was a peak of fifty-two public houses in Biggleswade in 1876 and seventeen still remain in the town.

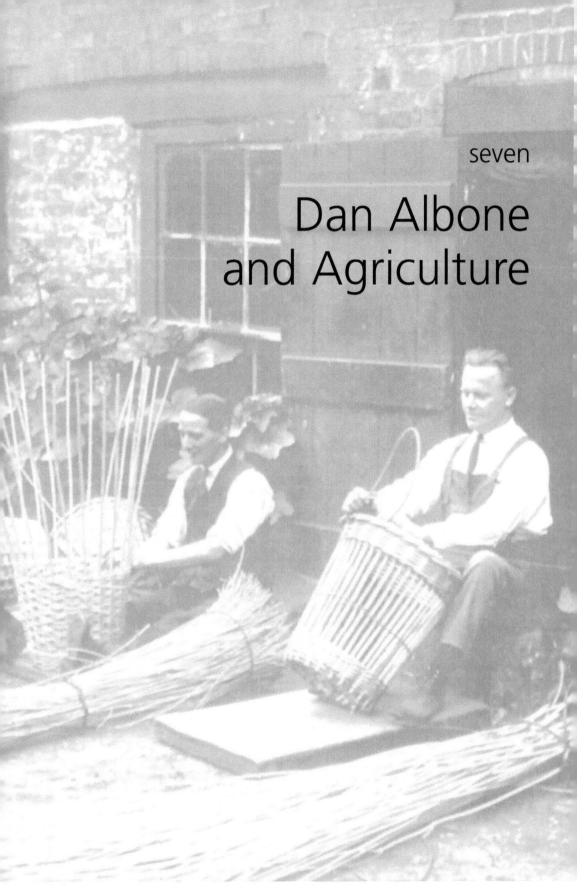

seven

Dan Albone
and Agriculture

Biggleswade's most famous son, Dan Albone (1860-1906). He was an inventor, pioneer, champion cyclist and publican.

Opposite above: Dan was born at the Ongley Arms in 1860 and was already making cycles at the rear of the pub when he took over the tenancy at the age of twenty-four.

Opposite below: Dan Albone at the Swiss Gardens, Old Warden, 1886. He had by then perfected his cross-frame bicycle, which could be ridden 'hands-off' and was termed 'the safety cycle'.

The Black Swan was rebuilt in 1886 as the Ivel Hotel, with the cycle factory behind. Dan Albone moved to the Ivel Hotel from the adjoining Ongley Arms.

By 1900 Dan was also building motorcycles and motor cars such as the Ivel Landaulet.

Dan designed and manufactured the first practical lightweight agricultural tractor, his most important invention, in 1902. The workforce is seen with Dan, who is on the right holding his baby daughter Alwyn.

There was great interest when the Ivel Agricultural Motor was demonstrated on a nearby farm in 1902. Dan is standing to the right, with his son Stanley.

The Ivel had many other uses apart from agriculture. It is seen here with a fire pump (*above*) and hauling a furniture van (*below*).

Dan Albone died suddenly in 1906 but his company continued until 1920. Both the Ivel Hotel and Ongley Arms (*right*) closed in 1918. The location of the Ivel Hotel and Ongley Arms was drawn specially by Jean Rainbow.

R.A. Jordan purchased both pubs, which were owned by different brewers. In 1956 they were also selling cars. The main building was the Ivel Hotel, with part of the Ongley Arms on the left. The buildings have all now been redeveloped.

Picking brussels sprouts in the 1920s. They were first grown here around 1900. Brusseling and cutting cabbages were mainly winter occupations, not recommended in frosty weather.

Packing and loading artichokes for the London markets in the 1920s.

A typical market gardener's cart dressed up for Biggleswade Fête, *c.* 1910.

Basket-makers used osier, a type of willow, which was cultivated in beds by the river Ivel. This scene from around 1900 shows workers cutting and peeling the tough flexible branches.

There were several basket-makers in Biggleswade. James Wells (*above*) of Hitchin Street stands outside his residence and workplace, *c.* 1910. Walter Wagstaff (*below*) is working in his Shortmead Street yard, with worker Fred Cooper, 1930.

Frederick Gee was born in 1843. He set up as a seedsman at the age of sixteen and prospered, moving to Riverford House in Shortmead Street, where this photograph was taken on 24 June 1887. His business closed in 1930. Riverford House was demolished in 2001 and the site is part of a new residential development.

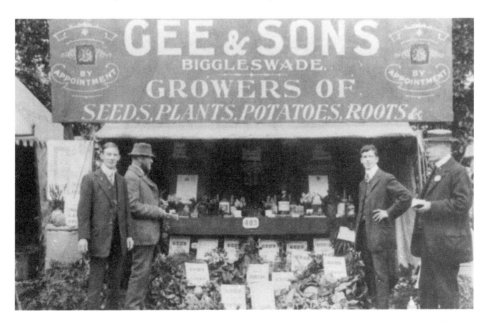

Frederick Gee (right) at Biggleswade Fête in 1910. Frederick supplied seeds to the royal farm at Windsor and was recognised as a royal seedsman by Queen Victoria. King Edward VII conferred a royal warrant, which was renewed by King George V.

These cottages at Frog Hall near Biggleswade were typical of farm workers' dwellings. A short walk from Brooklands Farm, they had basic facilities but were situated next to a stream.

Agricultural workers Fred Garner, Arthur Price, Fred Pepper and Bill Housden are enjoying their baver (lunch). This was quite often a Bedfordshire Clanger, a suet roll filled with meat and vegetables at one end and jam at the other. The bottles normally contained cold tea.

eight

Local Industry

John Maythorn started his coach-building business on a small scale in Sun Street in 1842 and moved to the Market Square around 1860. Twenty years later, John Maythorn and his employees are in front of the original showroom on the corner of Station Road and the Market Square.

This 1900 photograph shows the White Hart, the original Station Road showroom, John Maythorn's house, the new showroom and Brook House (now a supermarket).

Above and below: The dismal scene on 7 May 1923, the morning after a terrible fire destroyed the main Maythorn factory and left townsfolk in shock. Many workers feared for their jobs.

Reconstruction was completed in record time. The foreman and builders are seen here during the rebuilding of the main factory.

Two of the skilled craftsmen in 1925, using traditional ash to make coachwork for expensive limousines. By now the company was a subsidiary of Hooper's Coachbuilders Ltd of Dover Street, London.

A production line in the new factory in 1925, when the demand for traditional bodywork had declined, due to the Pressed Steel Co.'s new plant at Cowley. As the London works could cope with the reduced demand, Maythorn & Son Ltd closed down in 1931.

NURO films purchased the main factory in 1935, but closed in 1938. The NAAFI took over the premises from 1940 to 1958, followed by Delaney Gallay Ltd, who manufactured aircraft thermal insulation. They became Gloster Saro Ltd and finally Insumat Ltd. In 1990 the site was redeveloped into three shop units.

Above: Weatherley Oilgear Ltd moved into part of the Palace Street works in September 1939. They later moved to a new factory, seen here in 1958. The scrubland between the Dells Lane houses and the factory was the Humpty Dumpty meadow, which later became the north car park. The company became Weatherley Cincinnati in 1962, and a few years later Cincinnati Milacron. They closed in 1987 and the site was redeveloped for houses.

Berkeley Caravans Ltd was incorporated on 3 January 1947. Expansion was rapid and 650 workers downed their tools to fight a serious fire in 1951. Another fire in 1952 did not stop progress.

The 34ft Berkeley Governor-General and the 8ft Caravanette, just two of an extensive range produced that year, on display in 1953.

Opposite below: Shrager Brothers were repairing wartime aeroplanes at Old Warden in 1941. In 1946 they started to make caravans, moving to the extension of the wartime factory in Biggleswade vacated by Pobjoy Airmotors and Aircraft Ltd.

The company produced a new lightweight Berkeley Car in 1956. It was an immediate success and they were soon making one per hour. The company became overstretched and the last car was made in 1961. Jean Dye and Phyllis Glen (*above*) are taking a new car out of storage. Ian Mantle (*below*) is rallying a 492cc Berkeley which regularly outclassed competitors driving nominally more powerful cars.

Spong & Sons printing works was in Church Street. They were chemists and stationers, also producing *Spong's Almanack* yearly and the *North Beds Courier*. Printers are lined up outside the works in 1914, prior to the First World War.

Inside the printing works, typesetting was a laborious task which entailed fitting each letter into frames ready for the printing press.

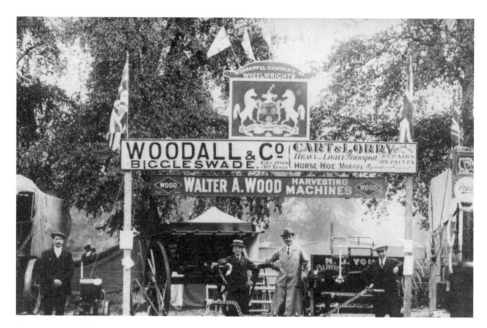

Samuel Woodall came to Biggleswade in 1861 to purchase a blacksmith's business in Shortmead Street. By 1921, when this photograph was taken at Biggleswade Agricultural Show, his son-in-law, Arthur Watkin, had purchased and expanded the business. A. W. Watkin stands centre right with his son Owen, who later took over the firm.

Watkin's garage in the 1930s, when they were agents for Singer cars. They steadily expanded their site but closed in 2000. The site is now a housing estate with roads named Watkin Walk and Woodall Close in recognition of the long-established business that once stood here.

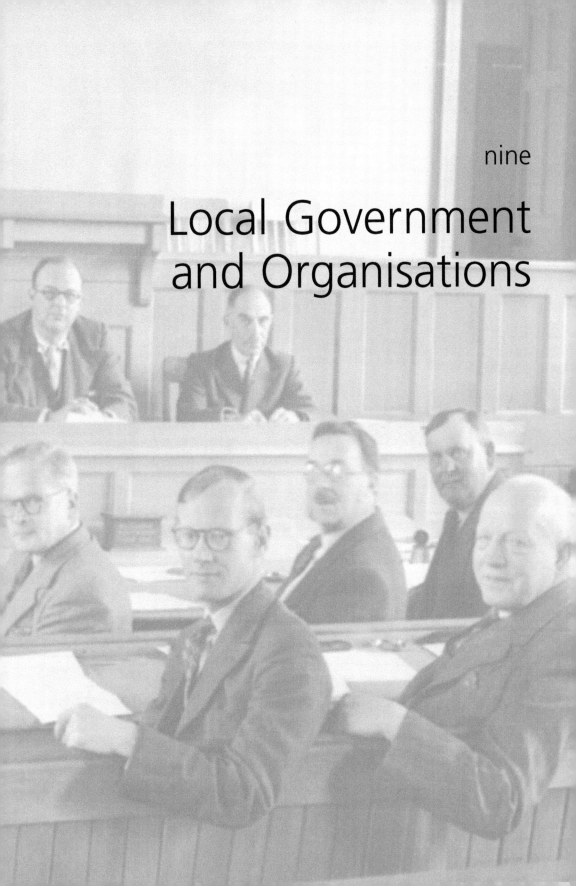

nine

Local Government
and Organisations

Biggleswade Urban District Council held their first meeting on 18 December 1894. Following the 1946 election, it is evident that there is only one young member.

There was another election in 1949, with members and officials of the urban district council holding their first meeting in the Magistrates Court.

A new council chamber opened in 1971. The chairman sits in the chair made especially for the UDC in 1897. With local government reorganisation, most powers were transferred to Mid-Bedfordshire District Council, leaving the town council with local responsibilities.

In 1869 the Local Burial Board opened the Drove Road cemetery, which had a chapel with a 90ft high spire. There were originally two chapels – one for the Church of England (on the right-hand side of the central spire) and the other for Nonconformists. The Church of England chapel is still available for use.

Biggleswade Board of Guardians was set up in 1834 under the Poor Law Act to administer the Union workhouse and Public Assistance. They eventually became redundant and had their last meeting in 1948.

Mrs Stevens, wife of the Chief Constable of Bedfordshire, presented the Biggleswade First Aid Squad of the St John Ambulance with certificates and medallions on 12 March 1936.

Civil Defence Workers at Stratton House take delivery of a new ambulance in 1940, a gift from the Canadian Red Cross.

Boys at Rose Lane Council School line up in the playground on 24 May 1918 for Empire Day. Old boys and soldiers on leave stand in the background.

A four-horse tender of Biggleswade volunteer fire brigade is on display in the Market Square, *c.* 1890. If there was a fire, horses were obtained from the Swan Hotel or the brewery.

The fire engine stands in front of the Swan Hotel. George Thomas, the landlord who supplied the horses, is holding the whip and his coachman, Gill Hutchins, stands on the right.

Biggleswade Town Band existed in 1893. Here, the Silver Prize Band is ready to play for Biggleswade Carnival in 1959; the band sadly disbanded some years ago.

The Market Square was thronged with horses and people for Biggleswade Horse Fair, a major event on St Valentines' Day, 14 February, for more than 300 years. There was still hustle and bustle in 1938, but the last fair was held in 1958.

With war clouds looming, local people and schoolchildren fill sandbags at the Public Assistance Institution (formerly the workhouse) in August 1939.

Thousands of children who had been evacuated from London arrived at Biggleswade railway station during the first three days of September 1939, nearly all in school groups wearing large labels. Many of these were housed with families in Biggleswade.

Prince Bernhard of the Netherlands visited Biggleswade Flower Show, organised by the Red Cross, in 1944. He is accompanied by Dudley Redman, Supt Gilbody and Alan Lennox-Boyd MP with his mother. On the left are Louie Cowles and Betty Munday.

On 12 May 1944, Lt-Gen. Franklyn, commanding the Home Forces, visited the Home Guard rifle range constructed in a former gravel pit at the Spread Eagle. The officers are lined up to meet him. The Commanding Officer, Lt-Col. Michael Bowes Lyon, the Queen's brother, is on the right.

Queen Elizabeth was invited by her brother to review the Home Guard at Fairfield on 23 July 1944. She is walking through the ranks accompanied by a retinue of commanding officers.

Later in 1944, the Home Guard stands down and 33 Platoon march along Fairfield Road led by the Platoon Commander, Harold Smith.

ten

Sport,
Leisure and
Personalities

Biggleswade Town football team – the Waders – are joined by their trainer and club officials at Fairfield and show grim satisfaction after winning the North Beds Challenge Cup for the 1909/10 season.

Biggleswade Thursday football club show their pride at winning their trophy in the Conservative Club garden.

Biggleswade Juniors at Fairfield in 1947. From left to right, back row: Charlie Maile, Ron Garnish, Jimmy Heath, Ron Smith, Phil Smith, Stan Godber, Alan Desborough. Front row: Porky Munns, Phil Smyth, Shooter Raybould, Bunny Munns, Dingle Mingay, George Wines.

Biggleswade ladies' cricket team with their gentlemen supporters make an attractive group at Fairfield around 1915.

Members of Biggleswade Caged Bird Society proudly hold their birds ready to show at the Memorial Hall, *c.* 1950.

Biggleswade Angling Club members display their trophies at the 1921 Annual General Meeting.

Housing estates now cover much of the area once used for skating on the river Ivel. Meadows were flooded to make ice rinks during Victorian and Edwardian winters. Special trains conveyed enthusiasts from London to Biggleswade.

At one o'clock on 11 March 1896, Lord George Sanger's circus paraded along the High Street. Mrs Sanger is enthroned on top of the Queen's Tableau, which is gilded with gold leaf.

Pupils outside Mrs Miller's Camden House School for Young Ladies in Crab Lane in 1894. They are staging a scene from Gilbert & Sullivan's comic opera *The Mikado*.

Enthusiastic pupils of Henry Keene's violin class are ready to perform at the Boys' Church School in 1936.

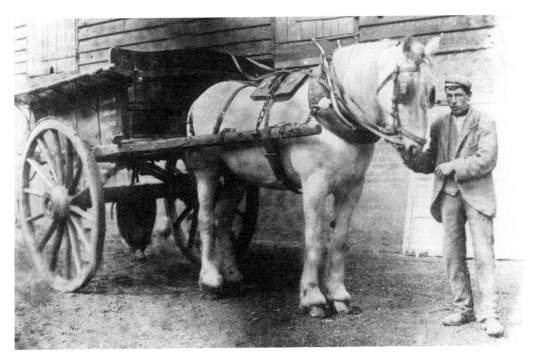

Jim Rawlings, a local merchant, with his horse and cart outside his storage barns in Back Street, c. 1910.

Ernest Kitchener of Langford Road was one of many dairymen delivering milk to local houses. Mrs Kitchener was also involved in the family business and their little daughter is joining in.

Isaac Smith relaxes in his local pub after a hot tiring day. Isaac was a well-known member of an old Biggleswade family and lived in a thatched cottage in Sun Street. His speciality was tarring wooden barns to make them weatherproof.

Opposite above: Baptist Sunday school pupils in the 1920s march into Frederick Kitchiner's meadow for their annual Sunday school treat, where they enjoyed sports and a slap-up tea.

Opposite below: The boys from Biggleswade Council School in Rose Lane won the Eastern Area athletics championship in June 1938. They are seen here with their headmaster and sports master outside the school.

William Housden, who died in 1939 aged ninety-three, was one of the last local cattle-drovers. He worked within a 30-mile radius of Biggleswade with his dog and hazel stick, driving herds of cattle from place to place or to market.

Alfred Wood started his career as a postman in 1887, retiring after forty-two years at the age of sixty. During his career, he earned the King's Imperial Service Medal and Diploma. He was also a Wesleyan local preacher and a part-time newspaper reporter.

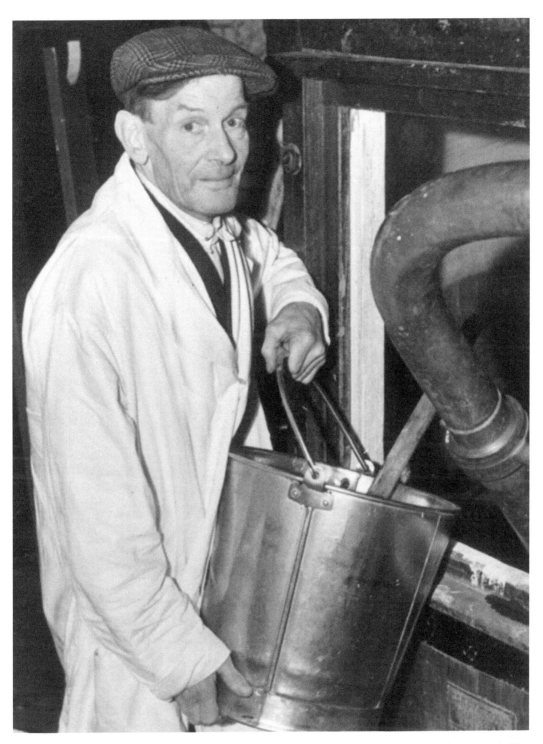

Charlie Daniels worked at Biggleswade Brewery from 1898 to 1950. At a presentation to mark fifty years' service with the company, he said that it was always his ambition to serve Messrs Wells and Winch for a long period!